A CourseGuide for

Know Why
You Believe

K. Scott Oliphint

ZONDERVAN
ACADEMIC

ZONDERVAN ACADEMIC

A CourseGuide for Know Why You Believe
Copyright © 2020 by Zondervan

Requests for information should be addressed to:
Zondervan, *3900 Sparks Dr. SE, Grand Rapids, Michigan 49546*

ISBN 978-0-310-11098-9 (softcover)

CONTENTS

Introduction

Welcome to *A CourseGuide for Know Why You Believe*. These guides
were created for formal and informal students alike who want to
engage deeper in biblical, theological, or ministry studies. We hope
this guide will provide an opportunity for you to grow not only in
your understanding, but also in your faith.

How to Use This Guide

This guide is meant to be used in conjunction with the book *Know
Why You Believe* and its corresponding videos, *Know Why You Believe
Video Lectures*. After you have read each chapter in the book and
watched the accompanying video lesson, the materials in this guide
will help you review and assess what you have learned. Application-
oriented questions are included as well.

Each CourseGuide has been individually designed to best equip
you in your studies, but in general, you can expect the following
components. Most CourseGuides begin every chapter with a "You
Should Know" section, which highlights key terminology, people,
and facts to remember. This section serves as a helpful summary for
directing your studies. Reflection questions, typically two to three
per chapter, prompt you to summarize key points you've learned.
Discussion questions invite you to an even deeper level of engage-
ment. Finally, most chapters will end with a short quiz to test your
retention. You can find the answer key to each quiz at the bottom of
the page following it.

For Further Study

CourseGuides accompany books and videos from some of the world's
top biblical and theological scholars. They may be used independently,

or in small groups or classrooms, offering quality instruction to equip students for academic and ministry pursuits. If you would like to engage in further study with Zondervan's CourseGuides, the full lineup may be viewed online. After completing your studies with *A CourseGuide for Know Why You Believe*, we recommend moving on to *A CourseGuide for Know How We Got Our Bible* and *A CourseGuide for Know the Heretics*.

Introduction to
Know Why You Believe

You Should Know

- The quotation from C. S. Lewis at the beginning of the introduction is from his lecture entitled "Is Theology Poetry?"

- One reason we ask the *why* question is that we want to understand things.

- The author writes that we can think of the Bible as the eyeglasses through which we see everything.

- Christianity does not have its primary source in nature; instead, its source is Jesus.

- Christianity encompasses the entire history of redemption before the time of Christ.

Essay Questions

Short

1. Do you believe it's important for Christians to think about why Christianity is true? Are there benefits to asking these questions? Are there consequences if we don't ask them? (p. 9–10)

2. How does your understanding of the Bible relate to your view of whether or how we should provide reasons for Christian beliefs?

3. Do you agree with the author that "Christianity is a way of seeing. It provides a foundation for everything we think, do, and believe"? Why or why not?

Long

1. What are some common objections to Christianity from non-believers? Should Christians try to answer these objections with reason and evidence? List 3 objections and how you would respond.

Quiz

1. _____ wrote, "I believe in Christianity as I believe that the sun has risen: not only because I see it, but because by it I see everything else."

   a) Martin Luther
   b) Saint Augustine
   c) C. S. Lewis
   d) The apostle Paul

2. (T/F) One reason we ask the question *why* is that we want a place of rest.

3. (T/F) According to the author, Christianity is a way of seeing.

4. (T/F) The Apostles' Creed describes the mode of Jesus's baptism.

5. The author compares the Bible to _____ through which we see everything.

   a) A kaleidoscope
   b) A microscope
   c) A periscope
   d) Eyeglasses

6. (T/F) The three primary sources for Christianity are nature, experience, and individual salvation.

7. (T/F) Christianity is properly understood by knowing and trusting in Jesus Christ.

8. (T/F) According to the author, evidence and argument are sufficient by themselves to convince someone to believe in Christianity.

9. The author states that the most important question throughout the book will be:

    a) "Do *I* believe this, and, if not, why don't I believe *this*?"
    b) "Who is Jesus, and how do I know him?"
    c) "What is the best argument for God's existence?"
    d) "How do I persuade people to accept Christ?"

10. (T/F) Only religious people have faith, while others rely on facts and evidence.

CHAPTER 1

Why Believe in the Bible?

You Should Know

- The Jewish historian Josephus wrote that Jesus was a man who did wondrous works and whose followers said he was the Messiah.

- After the New Testament, the second most documented work of ancient literature is Homer's *Iliad*.

- The Council of Nicea (325 AD) was called by Emperor Constantine to affirm the identity and full deity of Jesus Christ against the position of Arius and his followers.

- Believing that the Bible is true is more like being in a marriage relationship than like a scientific experiment.

- Because the Bible is the ultimate authority for Christians, there can be no other authority that can establish its authority.

Essay Questions

Short

1. What is your evaluation of the author's "external reasons" and "internal reasons" for believing the Bible? Do you find his evidence persuasive? Why or why not?

2. The author states that some people will object that he is arguing in a circle since he holds that the ultimate reason to believe the Bible is because of what the Bible says about itself. Is his defense of this "circular" reasoning persuasive? Whether you agree or disagree with the author, does "circular reasoning" automatically invalidate his case?

3. What is the best way to handle the objection that the Bible contains contradictions, and therefore can't be trusted? Do you find the author's response persuasive? Why or why not?

Long

1. The author quotes from Amazon.com reviews in which people claim that the Bible is racist, inaccurate, bigoted, and promotes slavery. Have you encountered these objections in conversations with nonbelievers? If so, how did you handle them? If not, how do you think you would respond?

Quiz

1. (T/F) The Bible is the bestselling book of all time.

2. (T/F) Like other religions, Christianity is the product of a private revelation.

3. (T/F) A recent archeological dig in Jerusalem discovered a seal belonging to the Old Testament king Hezekiah.

4. All of the following non-Christian writers except _____ refer to Jesus in their historical writings.

    a) Josephus
    b) Horace
    c) Tacitus
    d) Pliny

5. (T/F) The Dead Sea Scrolls contain copies of every book of the Old Testament except Esther.

6. There are more than _____ Greek manuscripts of parts or the whole of the New Testament.

    a) 5,000
    b) 10,000
    c) 25,000
    d) 50,000

7. (T/F) *The Da Vinci Code* by Dan Brown states that the Bible was assembled by the Roman emperor Constantine the Great.

8. (T/F) There was never a council called to decide which books to include in the New Testament.

9. (T/F) According to the author, historical evidence as such provides only probability, not certainty.

10. (T/F) The author contends that the only way to be assured of the divine authority of Scripture is for the Holy Spirit to testify to its truth in our hearts.

CHAPTER 2

Why Believe in God?

You Should Know

- Christopher Hitchens claimed that religion "*must* seek to interfere with the lives of nonbelievers, or heretics, or adherents of other faiths."

- Richard Dawkins wrote that "The God of the Old Testament is arguably the most unpleasant character in all fiction."

- John Calvin wrote that "There is within the human mind, and indeed by natural instinct, an awareness of divinity."

- General revelation is God's revelation that is constantly coming through all that he has made.

- One version of the cosmological argument states: "Everything that comes to be has a cause; the universe came to be; therefore, God caused the universe."

Essay Questions

Short

1. A number of atheists claim to follow Richard Dawkins in believing that our universe has "no design, no purpose, no evil, no good"—only "pitiless indifference." What are the implications of this worldview for how an atheist lives his or her life? Is this a worldview that seems conducive to human flourishing? Why or why not?

2. What do you think of John Calvin's view that human beings have an inborn awareness of divinity? If he's correct, why do so many people claim to be atheists or agnostics? In terms of evangelism or pastoral ministry, what is the best way to approach unbelief?

3. What do you think is the most compelling argument against God's existence, and why? What do you think is the most compelling argument for God's existence, and why?

Long

1. The New Atheists often make moral judgments about aspects of the Bible or Christianity that they find offensive. For those like Richard Dawkins who deny that objective morality exists, does this present a contradiction for their worldview? Is it necessary to presuppose God's existence to believe in objective morality (where "objective" means "true, regardless of any human's opinion")? Explain.

Quiz

1. All of the following are leaders of the New Atheism movement except
   a) Carl Sagan
   b) Sam Harris
   c) Richard Dawkins
   d) Christopher Hitchens

2. (T/F) The New Atheists claim that belief in a god is harmful to the flourishing of the human race.

3. The philosopher _____ claimed that "To such heights of evil are men driven by religion."
   a) Daniel Dennett
   b) Lucretius
   c) Friedrich Nietzsche
   d) Plotinus

4. (T/F) It is important to distinguish between what Christianity is and what people who claim to be Christians do.

5. The New Atheist writer _____ claims that the universe has "no design, no purpose, no evil, no good, nothing but pitiless indifference."
   a) Friedrich Nietzsche
   b) Carl Sagan

    c) Sam Harris

    d) Richard Dawkins

6. The _____ argument is based on Cicero's statement that "There never was any nation so barbarous, nor any people in the world so savage, as to be without some notion of Gods."

    a) Cosmological

    b) Paradoxical

    c) *Consensus gentium*

    d) Ecclesiological

7. (T/F) John Calvin held that all people possess an inherent knowledge of God.

8. (T/F) The inherent knowledge all people possess about God is sufficient to save them.

9. (T/F) Our "natural" knowledge of God includes the knowledge of what God requires of us.

10. (T/F) The philosopher Thomas Nagel confessed that he didn't want there to be a God and hoped there wasn't one.

CHAPTER 3

Why Believe in Jesus?

You Should Know

- The "Quest for the Historical Jesus" was an attempt to discover and write about the life of Jesus from a purely naturalistic point of view.

- *The Life of Jesus* by David F. Strauss was an attempt to recover the historical Jesus by rejecting any supernatural elements related to his life.

- The Dutch theologian Herman Bavinck wrote that "God's becoming human starts already immediately after the fall."

- The Princeton theologian Charles Hodge held that Christ was the Jehovah of the Old Testament.

- Theologian John Calvin argued that the angel that Jacob wrestled with in the Old Testament was Christ.

Essay Questions

Short

1. David F. Strauss in his *Life of Jesus* rejected any supernatural elements in Jesus's life, and accepted only "natural" events. In your opinion, is it acceptable for historians to accept the supernatural as an explanation of events in their historical work? Why or why not? (pp. 56–57)

2. Christians are sometimes accused of a contradiction when they claim Jesus is both God and man. Some question how anyone could be both. How would you respond if you were sharing the gospel with someone and this objection was raised?

3. What will happen, in your view, when Jesus comes again? What, in your view, are the main things Jesus wants to accomplish through his church before he comes again?

Long

1. If you were asked by an unbeliever to briefly describe who Jesus is, what would you say?

Quiz

1. (T/F) David F. Strauss in his book *The Life of Jesus* attempted to defend the historicity of Jesus's miracles and the validity of the gospel accounts.

2. (T/F) The Princeton theologian B. B. Warfield stated that Jesus was either divine or out of his mind.

3. (T/F) Jesus is both God and man.

4. Which of the following New Testament chapters presents Jesus as both God and man?
   a) 2 Corinthians 1
   b) 2 Thessalonians 1
   c) John 1
   d) Titus 1

5. (T/F) The Word described in John 1 is the second person of the Trinity.

6. The name *Jesus* is derived from the Hebrew name *Joshua*, meaning
   a) "Praise be to God"
   b) "Yahweh is salvation"
   c) "The Lord lives"
   d) "Grace and peace"

7. In one of his first synagogue appearances, Jesus stood up and read from
   a) Genesis 1
   b) Malachi 1
   c) Psalm 1
   d) Isaiah 61

8. (T/F) Jesus claimed to be the "I am" who met Moses on the mountain in Exodus 3.

9. (T/F) The Dutch theologian Herman Bavinck held that Christ is the mediator of both creation and re-creation.

10. (T/F) The angel that Jacob wrestled with in the Old Testament was most likely Gabriel.

CHAPTER 4

Why Believe in Miracles?

You Should Know

- Empiricism is the belief that we can know only what we experience through our senses.

- Naturalism is the view that only "natural" things can be known.

- Probability is the likelihood of something happening or taking place.

- David Hume defined a miracle as a violation of the laws of nature.

- C. S. Lewis contended that David Hume's argument against miracles was guilty of circular reasoning.

Essay Questions

Short

1. In your view, is it easier to believe that God exists, or that all that exists is nature? Please support your answer with two or three points.

2. What do you think of Hume's philosophy of empiricism? What are the pros and cons of an empirical approach to life?

3. According to the author, what was the purpose of the miracles God performed in the Bible? Do you agree that all the miracles in the Bible point to the "Grand Miracle" of the incarnation?

Long

1. What are the weaknesses of David Hume's argument against miracles? What are the weaknesses of Benedict de Spinoza's argument against miracles? In your view, does God still work miracles today? Why or why not?

Quiz

1. (T/F) C. S. Lewis wrote a book on miracles refuting David Hume and his followers.

2. (T/F) According to David Hume, any book on the topic of divinity would contain nothing but sophistry and illusion.

3. (T/F) David Hume believed that the testimony of eyewitnesses was enough to establish that a miracle had happened.

4. (T/F) The New Atheist Christopher Hitchens rejected Hume's arguments against miracles.

5. The Jewish philosopher _____ argued that miracles weren't possible because they would violate the unchanging laws of nature.
   a) Philo
   b) Aristotle
   c) Josephus
   d) Benedict de Spinoza

6. Miracles are not arbitrary displays of God's power, but _____.
   a) Point to the redemption that God accomplishes in Christ
   b) Signs that the end times have arrived
   c) Are powerful enough to convince any skeptic
   d) Are usually not reported by mainstream media

7. (T/F) According to the author, the manna in the Old Testament was meant to point to the true Bread that would bring eternal life.

8. (T/F) According to the author, all the miracles of the Bible are meant to point to the "Grand Miracle" of the incarnation.

9. (T/F) David Hume believed that only what could be experienced through the senses could be known.

10. (T/F) The author agrees with C. S. Lewis that if one assumes that God exists, the possibility of miracles occurring is more likely.

CHAPTER 5

Why Believe Jesus Rose from the Dead?

You Should Know

- Christian apologist Josh McDowell argued that the historical evidence for Jesus's resurrection "speaks for itself."

- Christian apologist John Warwick Montgomery wrote that the possibility of future evidence arising against the resurrection is "*almost too small* to be entertained."

- Nobel Prize winner Francis Crick suggested that aliens might be responsible for life on earth.

- "Death" in the Bible means an existence without fellowship and communion with God.

- Paul states that if the resurrection did not happen, then we should "eat and drink, for tomorrow we die."

Essay Questions

Short

1. Why did Jesus have to rise from the dead?

2. What do you think is the most significant objection to the resurrection? How would you respond to it?

3. What do we learn about Jesus' resurrection from Paul's description of it in 1 Corinthians 15?

Long

1. Why do Christians believe in the resurrection? How would you respond to Michael Martin's critiques of belief in the resurrection? If you were asked by a seeker why you believe in the resurrection, what would you say?

Quiz

1. (T/F) The earliest manuscript for Suetonius, who wrote about Caesar crossing the Rubicon, dates to almost a thousand years after Suetonius's death.

2. (T/F) Historical evidence can provide only probable, but not certain, conclusions.

3. (T/F) We all have basic commitments that force us to interpret facts in a certain way.

4. (T/F) The historical aspects of Christianity can be safely ignored.

5. (T/F) According to the author, historical data is sufficient to establish that Jesus rose from the dead.

6. (T/F) Paul's first letter to the Corinthians indicates that the resurrection is the central "key" that unlocks the whole of Christianity.

7. (T/F) There is no indication in the Old Testament that Christ would die and rise again.

8. (T/F) The Bible teaches that the resurrection of Christ is the beginning of one single "harvest" event.

9. (T/F) Atheist philosopher Michael Martin argues that Jesus's resurrection could be explained by future scientific discoveries.

10. (T/F) Atheist philosopher Michael Martin suggests that Jesus's disciples developed a belief in the resurrection based on religious bias.

ANSWER KEY
1. T, 2. T, 3. T, 4. F, 5. F, 6. T, 7. F, 8. T, 9. T, 10. T

CHAPTER 6

Why Believe in Salvation?

You Should Know

- The author points to Louis Zamperini's life as an illustration of the power of salvation.

- Sin can be defined as rebellion against God.

- The death that sin produces is not just physical death but eternal punishment.

- In order for the salvation that God has provided to be applied, we must believe in the Lord Jesus Christ.

- God sacrificed animals to cover Adam and Eve.

Essay Questions

Short

1. Why did God make garments of animal skin for Adam and Eve after the fall? What did these signify?

2. What does Hebrews 9:7–26 tell us about Christ's sacrifice?

3. What does it mean to "believe in Christ"? How has believing in Christ changed your life?

Long

1. According to Scripture, why do human beings need to be saved? If God is love, why doesn't he just forgive everyone who sins? Many

people in the West today believe that human beings are basically good. How would you respond to a non-believing friend who told you that?

Quiz

1. (T/F) Louis Zamperini reached a turning point in his life when he heard Billy Graham preach.

2. (T/F) Louis Zamperini had promised God that if God saved him, he would serve God forever.

3. (T/F) The Trinity isn't important when it comes to understanding salvation.

4. One meaning of being made in God's image is _____.
   a) That man has supernatural powers
   b) That man and woman have responsibilities given by God
   c) That we are also composed of three elements
   d) That we can one day recreate the Garden of Eden

5. (T/F) When Adam fell, so did the rest of creation.

6. Because Adam was designated as the representative of all human beings, _____.
   a) We should honor him as our ancestor
   b) We should strive to be like him
   c) His sin is credited to all of humanity after him
   d) We can justly blame him for all of our problems

7. (T/F) Since God is holy, he must punish all violations of his character.

8. (T/F) Sin requires the shedding of blood.

9. Scripture calls Christ "the last Adam" because _____.
   a) Unlike Adam, he obeyed perfectly
   b) He was the last of Adam's descendants
   c) He preached about all of Adam's failures
   d) He insisted that no one else should take Adam's name

10. The book of _____ informs us that Christ "entered the Most Holy Place once for all by his own blood, thus obtaining eternal redemption."

    a) Ecclesiastes
    b) Jude
    c) Acts
    d) Hebrews

CHAPTER 7

Why Believe in Life After Death?

You Should Know

- Christopher Hitchens believed that following death there would be nothing but "darkness."

- The Greek philosopher Plato believed that the soul was immortal.

- Naturalism is the belief that nothing except nature exists.

- The philosopher David Hume believed that human beings were just a "bundle of ideas" that died when the body died.

- Bishop Joseph Butler provided philosophical arguments for the afterlife in his book *The Analogy of Religion*.

Essay Questions

Short

1. Why do you think books about people visiting heaven are so popular? What is your opinion about near-death experiences? Do these tell us anything valuable about the afterlife?

2. What would you say to a skeptic you are sharing the gospel with who says he doesn't believe in an afterlife? If a church member asked what the Bible teaches about the afterlife, what would you tell him?

3. What evidence is there that people are more than simply material bodies? Why is it important for us to receive new spiritual bodies in the end?

Long

1. In your view, why do most Americans believe they will go to heaven when they die? What do you believe they are basing that belief on? How would you respond to the common objection that a loving God wouldn't send anyone to hell?

Quiz

1. _____ percent of Americans believe in an afterlife.

   a) 10
   b) 20
   c) 75
   d) 100

2. _____ percent of Americans believe they will go to heaven when they die.

   a) 82
   b) 5
   c) 25
   d) 100

3. (T/F) Books about people who die and visit heaven have not sold well recently.

4. Christianity and _____ are the two traditions most responsible for belief in the afterlife in the West.

   a) Zen Buddhism
   b) Greek philosophy
   c) New Age spirituality
   d) Popular culture

5. (T/F) It was Greek philosophy that made famous and familiar the notion of a "soul."

6. (T/F) The author believes that Bishop Joseph Butler made a successful case for the afterlife in his book *The Analogy of Religion.*

7. (T/F) The "Humanist Manifesto II" states that "The preciousness and dignity of the individual person is a central humanist value."

8. (T/F) The "image of God" meant that Adam and Eve were to work as God's servants and as lords over creation.

9. (T/F) One of the biblical images of heaven is people playing harps on clouds.

10. (T/F) The "image of God" has been defaced by the effects of sin.

CHAPTER 8

Why Believe in God in the Face of Modern Science?

You Should Know

- Natural philosophy referred to discovering the workings of the world and its benefits.

- Francis Bacon is credited with the application of the scientific method.

- The influential scientist Isaac Newton held that God, Providence, and theology were "central to any proper understanding of science and nature."

- The Enlightenment was an era in which thinkers of the day began to challenge all external authority.

- Punctuated equilibrium is the view that species changed so rapidly that there are few intermediate forms in the fossil record.

Essay Questions

Short

1. How did Francis Bacon, Robert Boyle, and Isaac Newton understand their scientific work in relation to God?

2. According to the author, why is evolution an incoherent theory? According to the author, in what way(s) does Christianity provide a foundation for science?

3. How should Christians respond to the Enlightenment view of human reason?

Long

1. In your view, is Christianity compatible with the modern scientific understanding of evolution? Why or why not? How do you understand the relationship between Christianity and science? Are they compatible, or incompatible? Why do you think so?

Quiz

1. (T/F) Modern science began in the nineteenth century.

2. (T/F) The word "scientist" wasn't coined until the nineteenth century.

3. (T/F) The Greek philosopher Thales accurately predicted a solar eclipse.

4. (T/F) The Christian chemist Robert Boyle concluded that the universe was the result of a random "concourse of atoms."

5. (T/F) The Age of Reason, or Enlightenment, sought to ground all truth in Scripture.

6. (T/F) John William Draper and Andrew Dickson White both wrote books arguing that religion was in conflict with science.

7. According to the author, the most influential book that pitted science against Christianity was _____.

   a) The Bible
   b) *The Origin of Species*
   c) Plato's *Republic*
   d) *History of the Conflict Between Religion and Science*

8. (T/F) For most people, "evolution" means a process of biological development guided by God.

9. (T/F) Christians blindly assume their position, while evolution is based on scientific evidence.

10. (T/F) The author believes that Richard Dawkins makes an effective moral argument against God's actions in the Old Testament.

CHAPTER 9

Why Believe in God Despite the Evil in the World?

You Should Know

- The Greek philosopher Epicurus defined the problem of evil in a series of questions about God and his character.

- The word theodicy refers to reasons or justification God would have for allowing evil.

- The "Greater Good Defense" tries to show that evil exists so that other virtues could exist and be apparent.

- "Free will" means that our choices are completely free of God's control.

- Theophany refers to an appearance or manifestation of God (e.g., in Genesis 3).

Essay Questions

Short

1. What is your evaluation of the "Greater Good Defense"? What are its pros and cons?

2. What is your evaluation of the "free will" response to evil? What are its pros and cons?

3. What do you believe is the relationship between God's sovereignty and human free will? According to Scripture, how did evil enter the world?

Long

1. If a church member asked you why there is so much evil in the world if God is loving, what would you say? What are some possible reasons God would allow a Christian to experience evil or suffering? Can you think of an episode of evil or suffering in your life that made you a better person? What happened, and how did it affect you?

Quiz

1. (T/F) According to the author, "evil" and "sin" are two words that mean the same thing.

2. (T/F) Philosopher Antony Flew's parable of "The Invisible Gardener" illustrated Flew's belief that God wanted to remain hidden from human beings.

3. (T/F) The author believes that the problem of evil motivated Flew's parable of "The Invisible Gardener."

4. (T/F) The Greek philosopher Epicurus proposed a series of solutions to the problem of evil.

5. (T/F) In the author's view, those who do not believe in God have no way of explaining what evil is.

6. To solve the problem of evil, one can deny each of the following attributes of God except _____.

    a) Omnipotence
    b) Omniscience
    c) Goodness
    d) Self-existence

7. Gottfried Wilhelm von Leibniz wrote a book on the problem of evil entitled _____.

    a) *Solving the Problem of Evil*
    b) *Theodicy*
    c) *Evil as I See It*
    d) *The Problem that Won't Go Away*

8. (T/F) Augustine believed that God created everything, including evil.

9. (T/F) Augustine believed that evil was not a thing, but a lack of a thing.

10. (T/F) The author believes that the best response to the problem of evil is "free will."

CHAPTER 10

Why Believe in Christianity Alone?

You Should Know

- In *The Closing of the American Mind* Allan Bloom argues that college students are unified in their relativism and in their allegiance to equality.

- "Relativism" means that truth is relative to the one who believes it.

- The essence of postmodernism is captured by the statement that "truth is whatever your peers will let you get away with."

- Religious pluralism means that in some way all religions are true.

- The writer Dostoevsky in *The Brothers Karamazov* wrote that if God does not exist, then anything is permissible.

Essay Questions

Short

1. What is the Buddhist parable of the elephant? How would you respond if a seeker told you he was persuaded by it?

2. Why do Christians believe Jesus is the only way to God? How would you respond to the common objection that it's arrogant and intolerant to claim there is only one true religion?

3. What do you think Dostoevsky meant when he wrote that if God does not exist, then anything is permissible?

Long

1. In what specific ways do you see relativism, religious pluralism, and tolerance playing out in society today? If one of the high school or college students in your church told you she didn't believe in objective truth, how would you respond?

Quiz

1. (T/F) According to Allan Bloom, every student entering the university today believes that truth is relative.

2. (T/F) According to the author, relativism is the "default" position people adopt when there is nothing outside of their own minds that they're willing to trust.

3. (T/F) The author holds that relativism is typically accompanied by belief in objective truth and intolerance.

4. (T/F) Today, tolerance means that I should recognize that you are as "right" about what you believe as I am.

5. (T/F) The truth of Christianity is not dependent on whether or not anyone believes it.

6. (T/F) The ultimate foundation of truth is God himself.

7. (T/F) The Buddhist parable of the elephant is correct to suggest that human beings are limited.

8. (T/F) The Old Testament has little to say about how God planned to redeem the world from sin.

9. (T/F) Christianity is the only religion that makes exclusive claims.

10. (T/F) Any religion that requires adherents to believe specific doctrines is intolerant.

Conclusion

You Should Know

- *The Lion, the Witch and the Wardrobe* by C. S. Lewis provides an illustration of how Satan questions God's authority.

- The term apologetics refers to the defense of the Christian faith.

- Every suppression of the truth is, by definition, a deception.

- The Westminster Confession of Faith states that our persuasion of the truth and authority of Scripture "is from the inward work of the Holy Spirit bearing witness by and with the Word in our hearts."

- According to 2 Corinthians 10:5, we should demolish arguments that set themselves against the knowledge of God.

Essay Questions

Short

1. What was the serpent's strategy in tempting Eve? Why was it effective? How does Satan use this strategy today?

2. What is the best way to handle objections to the Christian faith?

3. How does the Christian worldview make more sense of everything we see and experience than non-Christian worldviews? Please discuss two or three specific examples.

Long

1. What does the author mean when he says, "When we confess Christianity to be true, we are also confessing that anything that opposes Christianity is, by definition, false." What are some concrete applications of this principle?

Quiz

1. (T/F) To dispel doubts, Christians must recognize the authority of God's Word.

2. (T/F) The first thing that Satan attacked in the Garden was Adam and Eve's mental abilities.

3. Genesis tells us that the _____ was more crafty than any of the other animals.
    a) Human
    b) Fox
    c) Serpent
    d) Lion

4. (T/F) In Genesis 3, the serpent began with a question in order to persuade Eve to doubt God's authority.

5. (T/F) The serpent wanted to prevent Eve from knowing God better.

6. (T/F) In *The Lion, the Witch and the Wardrobe* by C. S. Lewis, Aslan agrees to die in Edmund's place.

7. Aslan's roar in response to the White Witch's question about his credibility indicates _____.
    a) That his word is bound up with his character
    b) That he was testing the White Witch's courage
    c) That he would talk with her again later
    d) That the lion is the king of the jungle

8. (T/F) According to the author, the only proper way to face the objections that come to us is by obtaining a seminary degree.

9. (T/F) If we confess Christianity is true, we are also confessing that anything that opposes Christianity is false.

10. (T/F) As the Spirit works in our hearts through God's Word, we move from unbelief to faith in Christ.

ANSWER KEY

1. T, 2. F, 3. C, 4. T, 5. T, 6. T, 7. A, 8. F, 9. T, 10. T

Notes

1. (T/F) To dispel doubts, Christians must experience the authority of God's Word.

2. (T/F) The text biographies Satan attributes to the Garden was Adam and Eve's memorial abilities.

3. Jennie tells us that the _____ was more crazy than any of the original finals.

   a. human _____
   b. Fox _____
   c. _____
   d. (T/F)

4. (T/F) Because Satan changed _____, suggestion in order to _____ persuade Eve to doubt God's authority.

5. (T/F) The serpent wanted to prevent Eve from eating God's better _____.

6. (T/F) In the book, the friend and the Mentor by C. S. Lewis, Adam appears in the "ground of Eden."

7. Adam's point in response to the White witch's freedom about his sin/nature was _____.

   a. that he wanted to run up with his brother.
   b. that he was repenting that, but with a change.
   c. that he would talk with her again later.
   d. that the logic in Eden of the angle.

8. (T/F) According to the author, the only proper way to read the whole Bible that came to reads by "starting a sanctuary dogma."

9. (T/F) If we confess Christianity is true, we are also comforting that _____ everything that proves is false.

10. (T/F) As the Spirit works in our hearts through God's Word, we move from unbelief to faith in Christ.

www.ingramcontent.com/pod-product-compliance
Lightning Source LLC
Chambersburg PA
CBHW011747020426
42331CB00014B/3304